BRITISH ROAD STEAM VEHICLES

BRITISH ROAD
STEAM VEHICLES

KENNETH BROWN,
R. C. RILEY
& ALAN THOMAS

Bramley Books

Front cover photograph: *An engine to be repatriated from Australia in recent times. Marshall road locomotive 52962 was exported new in 1909 via the firm's agents, R C Scrutton & Co Ltd of Sydney. It is pictured at the Great Dorset Steam Fair in 1992.*

Back cover photograph: *An engine which has twice seen extensive restoration is Clayton & Shuttleworth compound traction engine 48279 of 1919. Following exhibition at the Royal Show, she was sold to the Swimbridge Steam Threshing Co in Devon and worked in that county all her life. After many years lying abandoned at the bottom of a field, the present owner decided that she was worth the untold perseverance required to bring her back from the dead and "Phoenix", as she has been named, is indeed an engine which has risen from the ashes.*

Half title page photograph: *Sir W G Armstrong Whitworth & Co Ltd of Gateshead were one of the last companies to venture into steam road vehicle manufacture. During the 1920s they marketed a range of road rollers which met with limited success. Seven examples have survived the passing of time, including 10R19, a 10-ton example of 1924 which was new to Exeter Corporation in Devon, later passing to R Dingle & Sons Ltd of Stoke Climsland, Cornwall. Very heavily built machines, the cast rolls are a distinct feature. The positioning of the toolbox is unusual, being incorporated between the headstock and the chimney. Now preserved in Lincolnshire, 10R19 is finished in the livery of its first owners, Our picture shows it at the Netley Marsh Rally, near Southampton, in 1991.*

Title page photograph: *The sole-surviving example of a Foden showman's road locomotive is No. 2104 of 1910. "Prospector" spent its fairground career with William Shaw of Sheffield and was acquired in 1959 by one of Cornwall's pioneer preservationists, Dr Bob Dyke of Callington, who rallied it for many years. Today, it is numbered in the collection of Frank Lythgoe, Warburton, Cheshire and is pictured in his ownership at Bishops Castle, Shropshire, in 1986, standing close to one of the most authentically preserved steam roundabouts. Still steam operated and with organ playing in the centre, this set was once well known at fairs and rallies in ownership of Ashley Bros of Nottingham. It is now travelled by Notts preservationist, Jack Schofield.*

Photograph Acknowledgements:

Kenneth Brown: p51, p54.

Phyliss Pettitt: p5.

R. C. Riley: p6, p7, p9, p11, p12, p13, p14, p15, p16, p17, p18, p20, p21, p22, p23, p24, p25, p26, p27, p28, p29, p30, p31, p32, p33, p34, p35, p36, p37, p38, p39, p40, p41, p42, p43, p44, p53, p58, p60, p61, p62, p63, p64, p98-112.

Alan Thomas: Front and back cover, half title page, title page, p10, p19, p45, p46, p47, p48, p49, p50, p52, p55, p56, p57, p59, p65, p66, p67, p68, p69, p70, p71, p72, p73, p74, p75, p76, p77, p78, p79, p80, p81, p82, p83, p84, p85, p86, p87, p88, p90, p91, p92, p93, p95, p96.

First published in Great Britain in 1999 by
Collins & Brown Limited
London House
Great Eastern Wharf
Parkgate Road
London SW11 4NQ

Text copyright © Collins & Brown Limited

This edition produced by Collins & Brown for Bramley Books,
an imprint of Quadrillion Publishing Ltd

British Library Cataloguing in Publication Data:
A CIP catalogue record for this book is available from the British Library.

ISBN 1 - 84100 - 348 - 4

Creative director: Julian Holland
Designed by Nigel White
Origination by Colour Symphony
Printed in China

HISTORICAL BACKGROUND

Centuries hence, historians will look back on the steam era – the time when steam provided the prime source of power – as extremely short. Starting early in the 18th century with the crude atmospheric pumping engines of Thomas Newcomen, it peaked in the 19th century with the coming of railways and then began to tail off. It will probably end early in the next millennium when the steam turbine for generating electric power is finally superseded.

Compared with these 300 years, the spell enjoyed by steam for road haulage and agricultural work was even shorter. It took a long time to get started in the mid-19th century due to the cumbersome nature of early steam engines and their separate boiler plants. No wonder Matthew Murray, a prominent Leeds industrialist, observed that the steam engine was about as portable as a parish church! It needed railway engines to point the way, yet in the earliest designs of traction engine, railway influence soon disappeared. The next approach was to adapt the horse-towed portable engine, where the cylinder and motion were carried on top of the boiler, to enable the engine to move itself along.

By the 1880s, the three principal variants had become established: the agricultural traction engine, forerunner of the farm tractor; the road locomotive, more refined, for heavy haulage on the roads, and the steam roller. All three were built in varying numbers until the 1930s, and a few later, together with the non-self-propelled portable engine. The lineage of the steam waggon, or lorry, on the other hand, was much less clearly defined. Its popularity peaked for only about 20 years and exhibited considerable variety in design. Halfway through the present century commercial steam on the road was dead. It had always suffered from its inherent weight and punitive legislation, but what finally killed it off was the internal combustion engine. Only the humble steam roller, whose weight was a positive asset, continued in use into the 1960s. The era of commercial steam on the road lasted a mere 100 years.

However, though it was completely unforeseen, a new road steam era was dawning – the preservation era. It was kick-started in 1950 by two steam worthies challenging one another to a traction engine race. In hindsight, the move is seen to have been inevitable as steam devotees saw that owning a traction engine was within their purse. Veteran car owners had already led the way. The only difference with a traction engine was that one needed more space to keep it, different skills to drive and maintain it, and it used solid fuel. It could also explode if not properly managed but there were plenty of retired steam drivers around to advise the novice (such a disaster to an engine in preservation has fortunately never happened).

The preservation movement was helped by the large number of engines lying derelict in yards all over the country. Indeed, during the Suez oil crisis in 1956 it was estimated that there were some 800-900 road steamers that could be put back into service at a pinch. Some steam rollers passed directly into preservation without a spell of rusting deterioration – the first engine owned by one of the authors came into this category. 'Steam meets' where engine owners would bring their engines together for a social steam-up became popular in the 1950s – indeed they still are – but it was quickly seen that they could be commercialised by inviting the public. Some cash

This steam party, arranged informally by a few enthusiasts, is typical of the start of the preservation movement. It took place near Camborne, Cornwall, in 1955. Almost unbelievably, one of the engines present was scrapped soon after because it needed heavy repairs!

To see an engine at work conveys to the uninitiated a living portrayal of the use to which it was once put. Burrell single cylinder traction engine 4048, a late example built in 1926, can be seen on the belt to a Ransomes threshing machine at the 1971 Horsham Rally. The arrangement of the footplate with such components as reversing lever (extreme right), regulator, steering wheel, pressure gauge and boiler feed pump can be clearly seen. "William the Second" was new to a Norfolk owner but also spent several years at work with Hampshire threshing contractor, William Hillary of Micheldever, before entering preservation.

would then be available to reward engine owners and the whole movement boosted. Forty years on, some people think that engine rallies have become over-commercialised. But their continuing popularity among the public and the pleasure that engine owners get from showing off their charges will ensure their continuance for many years to come.

Considerable changes in rally operation have occurred since the early days. The Grand Parade is still popular but engines are never raced due to the risk of damage and possible injury. Today, manoeuvrability and tests of skill have come to the fore, along with demonstration areas where engines can be put to the use for which they were designed. What more satisfying sound to a roller driver is there than the crunch of hardcore beneath the steel treads? Rallies vary greatly in size but easily the biggest event on the traction engine calendar is the Great Dorset Steam Fair held annually over the five days from Wednesday to Sunday following the Late Summer Bank Holiday. Originally sited at Stourpaine, near Blandford Forum, in recent years it has been held at Tarrant Hinton nearby, and attracts upwards of 200 engines and wagons, plus other steam exhibits.

Another thing that has changed since the early days is the price one has to pay for an engine, such is the law of supply and demand. In the 1950s an engine could change hands for £25. Today a good engine in working trim will probably set one back by five figures; only the more common types of steam roller can be had for less. A fairground type road locomotive with all the embellishments may well auction for six. This price hike makes it difficult for the younger enthusiast wishing to enter the ownership stakes. But as part compensation, steam engines are very labour intensive – one of the reasons for their demise – and most owners will gladly accept help. And hard work is not only demanded whilst an engine is in steam, there is also the annual chore of winter maintenance.

Another aspect of the preservation era is the more safety-conscious society we are becoming. Steam boiler insurance, backed by a searching examination each year by a qualified inspector, is of extreme importance. An explosion in the presence of the public could be catastrophic. Today, repairs to the boiler have to be carried out professionally and one effect of both traction and railway engine preservation movements is that firms specialising in such work have sprung up. Some owners prefer to contract the complete restoration of an engine to 'as new' condition, though the majority like to do as much work as possible themselves. Maintaining and insuring an engine is expensive and some owners, faced with major boiler repairs, prefer to keep the engine off the road while they save up. This ensures a regular turnover of engines on the rally fields, so no organiser can be accused of displaying all the same engines, year after year. Besides which, using low-loaders, engines can now be transported considerable distances.

The original sources of derelict engines in this country having virtually dried up, an increasing number is being imported from overseas. It means that a few engines of unfamiliar manufacture can now be seen at rallies. In some of our former colonies there are many derelict engines of British make, notably in Australia, though that country has recently tightened its export restrictions. At a conservative estimate there are currently in excess of 3,000 engines and steam wagons in this country, though not all in running condition.

Driving a steam engine of any kind is a fully rewarding experience as anyone who has ever wanted to be a railway engine driver will tell you. Handling one on the road is always a challenge with, besides the proper selection of the gears and steering effort needed, other traffic, the state of the fire and water level in the boiler all need constant attention. The good driver is the one who can match the amount of steam being produced to the work being performed, without either running short of steam or allowing wasteful discharge through the safety valves.

The high degree of 'job satisfaction' attended with steam, coupled with facilities which are now capable of building new engines, should ensure that steam may be seen, heard and smelt in action on the road far into the foreseeable future. That is, always assuming that European legislation never succeeds in driving it off the road: there have been some ominous noises. Certainly today's traffic conditions make driving an engine along the road more difficult. Mini-roundabouts, pedestrian studs, parked cars and cat's eyes are particularly hostile, especially to a roller, which is unsprung and has a wide steering lock. It is ideal for producing a 'do-it-yourself' traffic jam! At the other end of the scale, the 1930s steam lorry can not only keep up with traffic in a built-up area but beat almost anything away from traffic lights!

There are local clubs for traction engine enthusiasts all over the country and it is generally these that organise the 100 or so rallies that take place every year. There is also the National Traction Engine Trust, the official umbrella organisation to which most local clubs are affiliated. Apart from helping with legal and technical matters, the Trust keeps an eagle eye on any new legislation which could constitute a threat to what is a most rewarding hobby.

The photographs of preserved engines and wagons in this book were nearly all taken at rallies and cover the whole of the relevant period. They have been carefully selected to show a large range of types, including the humble portable engine from which it all began, and to illustrate examples of both rare and common makes. Two of the authors live in Cornwall and make no apology if there is a slight preponderance of West Country scenes.

Many examples of steam rollers have survived to preservation as this class of engine was commercially used long after other types had been taken out of use. Sadly, a number have in more recent times been converted to a status that they never should have been. Such has been the case with Fowler 17470, an 8-ton example, since she was pictured here at Hadlow Down, Sussex in 1970, participating in the grand parade during a sunny summer's afternoon. Here she is seen in the form in which she was supplied new in 1928 to Horsham Rural District Council.

GENERAL DESCRIPTION

The great majority of traction engines, road locomotives and steam rollers that ran on Britain's roads are of the same basic form, shown in the diagram on page 8. A dominant feature which distinguishes them from other forms of steam engine is that the horizontal boiler also serves as the main frame. Front and rear axles are attached to it while the engine unit is mounted on top. Only the hind wheels are driven. A train of gears provides the necessary speed reduction between the crankshaft and the axle, with a change speed device by which the gear ratio can be changed according to the work being performed. A neutral position enables the motion to run free, or drive machinery by flat belt from the flywheel.

The hind wheels are usually of the order of 5-6ft diameter and provided with broad treads. Engines likely to be used on soft ground, such as for farm work, have ridges, or strakes, on the rear treads for better grip. Road locomotives and others used only for road haulage have solid rubber tyres, while rollers have smooth treads. The front wheels are attached to a steerable front axle, or forecarriage, pivoted beneath the smokebox while a steam roller has front rolls carried in a forked casting. This pivots in a cast headstock which projects in front of

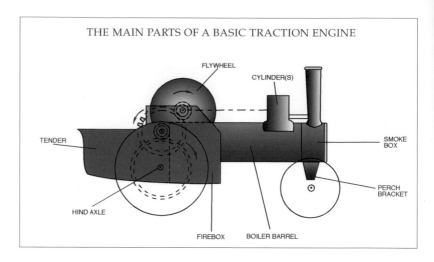

THE MAIN PARTS OF A BASIC TRACTION ENGINE

the smokebox and incorporates the base of the chimney. A few engines were made convertible with provision for attaching a bolted-on steering head and substituting smooth rolls for wheels.

In order to carry its own water and coal and provide a footplate for the crew, an engine has a tender bolted to the rear of the boiler. It consists of a riveted or welded steel box to contain water, with upswept sides and rear to form a coal box. The driver (and steersman if one is needed) stand on the tank top, between the coal box and the boiler. The fire door through which coal is fed into the firebox is in front of the driver's feet.

Most engines employ an ingenious patent (by Thomas Aveling, founder of the firm Aveling & Porter, in 1870) whereby the outer firebox side plates are extended upwards and rearwards beyond the profile of the boiler to carry the bearings for the crankshaft, intermediate gear shafts and hind axle, and to which the tender is bolted.

The single or compound cylinder(s) are arranged in a common cast block incorporating a steam jacket and shaped for a snug fit to the boiler top. It also includes the valve chest(s) and steam throttle valve, and carries connections for the safety valves, cylinder lubricator, speed governor (for work on the belt) and whistle. To the rear of it are bolted the guide(s) for the piston rod crosshead(s). Attached to the sides or top of the boiler are connections for cold water feed from one or two steam injectors, and/or a feed pump driven from the crankshaft.

The driver's controls are extremely simple – a throttle lever, forward/reverse lever, steering wheel (for the worm-geared chain steering), handbrake and levers or handwheels controlling the boiler feed equipment and cylinder drain taps. There are also levers for gear selection – only operated when the engine is stationary – which give a choice of two speeds, or for a road locomotive, three. Somewhere near the footplate will be a steam cock for the water lifter (used when taking water from a tank or stream) and some engines have a flywheel brake in addition to the parking handbrake. The brakes, incidentally, are mainly used for retardation going downhill and for parking. Lastly, there is a rod for working the ashpan damper which controls air to the grate.

Instrumentation is even simpler: a steam pressure gauge and a pair of sight glasses showing the water level in the boiler. The level in the tank is checked by dipstick. On the level a traction engine or roller with two speeds should be able to travel at between 5 and 7 miles on a tankful, depending on whether a load is being hauled, at a speed of 5-6 mph. Road locomotives with three speeds can travel much faster, perhaps 12-15 mph, and their range is extended by having an additional water tank slung under the boiler barrel – a 'belly tank'. Such engines also have crude springing to both axles and, in an effort to reduce the frightening effect on horses, a solid flywheel instead of spokes and cover plates each side of the motion. The two last-named features were also applied to rollers but for obvious reasons these are unsprung.

Traction engines and road locomotives are normally provided with a winch drum inside one of the hind wheels enabling them to haul themselves out of a sticky patch using a wire rope anchored to something solid – perhaps a tree or another engine. Clutching the drum in and the wheels out is done by drive pins which reach in through the wheel hubs. In the same way, the differential gear can be locked so that both hind wheels revolve together, another useful feature for soft ground. Most rollers lack both drum and differential, and for rounding sharp corners, removal of one of the drive pins will leave the wheel on that side free on the axle. However, driving on only one wheel is very risky on hills: with a smooth tread a roller can easily start to slide.

Questions often asked of engine owners are, how long does it take to raise steam and how much coal does it burn? Both depend on the quality of the coal and skill of the driver. Lighting the fire is done using wood laced with paraffin, sump oil or diesel, then coal is fed in gradually until the whole area of the grate is covered with burning fuel. The engine should have enough steam to move in one to two hours. Fuel consumption thereafter depends very much on the work being performed.

Some engines have a roof, or canopy, to protect the crew in wet weather, but this was not always thought necessary. It is certainly easier to attend to all the oiling points without one as they can be seen better. A feature which intrigues some people is that in some engines the flywheel revolves in the same direction as the road wheels, while in others it goes the opposite way. This depends on the number of shafts and gears in the drive train. The diagram depicts a three-shaft engine; that is, there is one intermediate gear shaft between the crankshaft and hind axle, so the crankshaft and wheels revolve in the same direction. Four-shaft engines have two intermediate gear shafts, then the directions of rotation are opposite. The latter arrangement loses a little more power due to friction but offers important advantages in layout, particularly in the change speed gearing.

Portable Engines

The most obvious variant on the basic traction engine theme is the portable engine. These were somewhat slow in entering the preservation stakes since they are less fun to handle, nevertheless they are of historic importance. Being confined to working on the belt they have no footplate, tender, driven wheels or gears, and the person tending them simply stands on the ground. A tank full of water is needed from which to top up the boiler.

The cylinder block, motion, crankshaft and flywheel are usually top mounted like a traction engine but arranged the other way round with the cylinder(s) over the firebox for better heat efficiency. The crankshaft is commonly provided with a belt pulley of smaller diameter than the

This example of a Burrell traction engine is of the single crank compound design, making use of a single crank and compound cylinders for more economic use of the steam. No. 2933 was new in 1907, spending its working life in East Anglia and later in Devon before passing into preservation in Hampshire. Burrells were built at Thetford, Norfolk and a distinctive feature of the make is the elegant flared copper top fitted to the chimney. The governor, which regulates the flow of steam whilst the engine is on the belt, can be seen mounted on the cylinder block.

An example of a portable engine which started it all! Richard Hornsby of Grantham was an early engine builder, producing mainly portables along with a few traction engines. Illustrated is single cylinder portable 3444, a veteran of 1878, particularly interesting as it has the cylinder enclosed in an upward extension of the firebox and is also mounted on wooden wheels. The inclined boiler pump can also be seen, with suction hose feeding from a barrel of water. It spent much of its working life powering a sawmill at Longhope, Glos and is preserved not too far away. It is pictured at a special gathering of portable engines at the Great Dorset Steam Fair in 1995.

flywheel, for drive purposes. A pump and sometimes an injector are provided for filling the boiler using a flexible suction hose from the tank. A tall chimney extension which folds down for travelling is also a normal fitment: it improves the draught on the fire as well as keeping sparks well clear of anything combustible in the vicinity.

Portable engines were used for a wide variety of work other than driving agricultural machinery. This included driving stone crushers in quarries, pumps and hoists in mines, sawmills, and machinery in small factories: indeed in any situation where work did not justify the capital cost of a fixed installation. Belting one up to a stone crusher or a sawbench makes an interesting display at a rally. It is thrilling to hear the deep chuffs from the chimney when the load suddenly comes on!

When greater power was needed a semi-portable engine was sometimes seen as the solution. This was a larger-than-normal portable engine whose wheels were only used for manoeuvring into position, then they were removed and the engine became a fixed installation. It often had enough power to drive a generator in addition to its main duty. Semi-portables were commonly found in quarries and sawmills; in the latter offcuts and sawdust provided most of the fuel needs.

It was the portable engine that gave rise to the nominal horsepower (nhp) classification of traction engines and road locomotives. In the early days it was the number of horses needed to tow an engine, and the practice stuck, even though to obtain the indicated horsepower one had to multiply by about six. Steam rollers were classified by weight. For example, a 10-ton roller is equivalent in boiler and cylinder capacity to a 6nhp traction engine.

It will be evident from the foregoing that unlike other forms of prime mover, a steam engine's design is skilfully adapted to the work it has to perform: after all. a petrol engine looks pretty much the same whatever it does. The adaptability of a steam engine is nowhere more evident than in the specialist types of portable engine built for the fairground. While a detailed description is outside the scope of this book, a few tasters follow.

The electric light engine is little more than a normal portable engine fitted with a dynamo, partly cased in and with due embellishment. The centre engine for a set of steam yachts (steam swingboats) also looks like a normal portable engine on pneumatic tyres. However, there is no flywheel because the twin crankshafts never perform more than half a turn. When the ride is built up the engine stands between the two swingboats, linkage from the ends of the crankshafts being connected to overhead shafting from which the swings depend. As the pistons reciprocate to and fro, the motion is this imparted to the swingboats, the travel being built up gradually from rest by the skill of the driver working the valves manually.

Other types of centre engine have no wheels of their own and are built into the ride that they drive. A galloper centre engine, for example, has a short, squat boiler which enables it to be mounted transversely at one end of the centre truck on which the 'centre pole' of the roundabout is mounted. Shafting and gears transmit motion to the rotating top from a small twin high-pressure cylinder engine unit on top of the boiler and the exhaust is led up the centre pole to emerge at the top. A fixed water tank beneath the boiler has to be topped up from tanks concealed beneath the platform when the ride is running. As a matter of interest, the top gearing and bottom slide by which the horses receive their galloping action were patented by Frederick Savage of Kings Lynn. His firm not only built traction engines but also invented a number of devices associated with the fairground.

A number of centre engines have found their way into preservation, either divorced from the ride or built back into a machine to restore steam operation. Some gallopers today are capable of being operated by steam or electricity, the latter being much more convenient at a normal funfair though of course needing a power supply. The so-called steam organs which accompany these lovely old rides use air as the operating medium like a church organ. The bellows or blower which supplies the air under pressure was traditionally belt driven from a small vertical engine mounted on the centre engine smokebox, always called the 'model' but today it is usually done by a small electric motor. In a steam switchback the arrangement of the centre engine was somewhat different, and the model stood to one side.

Other Variants

The road locomotive has an important variant, the steam tractor. This is simply a road locomotive scaled down so as to come within a specific weight limit for road tax purposes. The 5-ton tractor was the most common and was produced by a number of manufacturers, though 7.25-ton designs were also evolved. It was always difficult to get an engine down to the specified weight and many stories are told of the tricks indulged in by manufacturers when a new design was subject to the scrutiny of a government inspector. Invariably the engine was empty of coal and water and sometimes items like firebars and chimneys were made of wood! Inspectors soon got wise to this sort of trick and insisted on the fire being lit in their presence!

A variant of the agricultural traction engine is the ploughing engine. The largest engines to be made, they carry a horizontal wire rope drum beneath the boiler. The top of the drum is cast in the form of a gear wheel which engages a smaller gear wheel affixed to a vertical shaft driven by a set of bevel gears from the crankshaft at its upper end. Ploughing engines usually worked in pairs, positioned one each side of a field. The wire rope from each engine was attached to either end of the implement used, the latter then being drawn across the field by the engine effecting the 'pull'. At the end of the pull, the driver of the engine nearest the implement gave a blast on the whistle, this being the signal for the partner engine to draw the tackle back across the field. A crew member was required to 'ride' the implement in order to steer it on a regular course. Implements included ploughs, cultivators and various forms of harrow. The two-engine system was also used for mole-draining and dredging of lakes. Ploughs comprised two sets of shares which could be raised and lowered according to the direction of travel. They were designed to plough up to six furrows at a time and were thus much more efficient than the previously used single furrow horse-drawn ploughs.

Steam waggons or lorries varied so much in form that the reader is referred to the photographs and individual descriptions, or one of the standard works on steam vehicle design. Their concept might be traced back to Frenchman Cugnot's 3-wheeled steam carriage of 1769 or Richard Trevithick's pioneer road locomotive of 1801, though modern steam vehicles owe very little to these early freaks. Foden and Sentinel both produced tractors as a shortened form of their steam lorries, and these proved handier in awkward situations, such as tree-felling, than their road-locomotive based counterparts.

The London to Brighton Run attracts a number of steam vehicles annually. At Streatham Hill in 1975 can be seen Sentinel Super type waggon (the firm always spelled waggon with a double "g") 8393 of 1930. Sentinel adopted the undertype design, using a vertical boiler and an engine mounted between the chassis frames. The Super had a single speed and was constantly in gear. It used chain drive to the rear axle. 8393 was new to Wm Brown & Co of Ipswich, Suffolk, and has been widely rallied for many years by HMS Sultan, the Royal Naval Marine Engineering School, of Gosport, Hants, travelling everywhere under its own steam.

"Old Timer", Marshall single cylinder traction engine 37690 of 1902, is charged with the responsibility of having given birth to the road steam preservation movement. Back in 1950, her then (and now) owner, Arthur Napper, who lived in the Berkshire village of Appleford, challenged a neighbouring engine owner to a race with their respective engines, the winner to be the recipient of a firkin of ale. The event attracted overwhelming publicity and support. "Old Timer" duly won the race and the traction engine rally was born. Over the years, flat-out racing of engines was to give way to more sedate parades and working demonstrations, rallies being held the length and breadth of the country, providing entertainment for many thousands throughout the summer months. "Old Timer" is pictured at Crystal Palace in 1959.

During the pioneer days of preservation most engines travelled to and from rallies under their own power. Pictured on arrival at Andover in May 1955 is Fowler showman's road locomotive 15319 "Queen Mary" which was supplied new in 1918 to the War Dept as a haulage engine. After a period hauling stone for a Dorset quarry owner, she was acquired by Weymouth amusement caterers, Richard Townshend & Sons and rebuilt for use on the fairground, a dynamo being mounted on a platform in front of the chimney and the canopy, supported by decorative twisted brass columns, extended accordingly. An early preservation project, she has been regularly rallied for over 40 years.

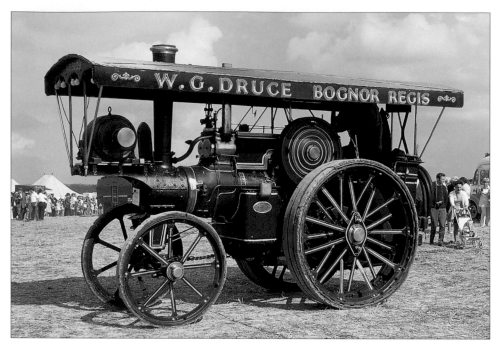

Above: *An engine that was purchased new by the War Office for use as a gun haulage tractor in 1909, Fowler 11799 is a rare survivor of its class (E1). Originally a triple expansion type, it was fitted with a third cylinder, the latter being removed later in life. It also experienced several years on the fairground in the ownership of Hampshire showman, Nelson Noyce, whose family still travel the tobers today with a galloping horse roundabout (illustrated on page 44). The engine was frequently to be seen at rallies from the 1950s with her first preservation owner and is pictured at Horsham in 1970.*

Right: *When pictured at Crystal Palace in September 1959, Aveling & Porter 15-ton roller 2185, a veteran of 1886, was still at work for its original owners, Croydon Borough Council. It shows several typical design features of the day, the massive headstock supporting the front roll and wide diameter of boiler barrel being very much in evidence. The brightly painted flywheel and front roll fork, however, would not be regular practice. The roller still survives, being part of the Science Museum's reserve collection at Wroughton, near Swindon.*

Above: *To cope with the electricity demands of the smaller fairground attractions, many steam tractors were adapted to serve with the addition of smokebox extension and dynamo. Some, like Burrell 'Gold Medal' tractor 3497 "May Queen" illustrated above, also saw a change to pneumatic-tyred front wheels during their final years in service. New as a standard haulage tractor, this particular example was rebuilt for use on the fairgrounds in ownership of Miss Sally Beach of Uxbridge, Middx, entering preservation in the early 1950s and is pictured at Crystal Palace in 1959. The name was taken from the steam centre engine on the firm's roundabout. Today, she has reverted to her original tractor status.*

Right: *Early steam rallies were much more relaxed affairs than their present day counterparts. Engines arrived on the day of the show (usually a Saturday), entertained their public for a few hours during the afternoon, then departed for home. Enthusiasts who can remember them do so with great nostalgia. Such an event would have been Paddock Wood, Kent, in August 1957. The general public enjoy a close inspection of the engines before events get underway. Pictured are (left) Clayton & Shuttleworth traction engine 36336 of 1904 and a 1925 Burrell compound 4019. The latter is unusual for a traction engine in being fitted with a disc flywheel, this normally being found on road locomotives and rollers. The sacks contain coal for the engines, usually supplied by the event organisers.*

Left: *A delightful study of a working steam roller in its twilight years. Pictured in Exeter, Devon, in July 1957, Aveling & Porter 10510, an 8-ton piston valve single of 1923, had spent the whole of its life at work with the Eddison Plant Ltd of Dorchester, a company which, over the years, owned what was the largest commercial fleet of steam rollers in the country. The canopy with scalloped front cross-member and galvanised roof are typical Eddison trade marks, as are the steam uptake pipe from the cylinder block and fleet number attached to the front of the headstock. This roller exists today, albeit in very different circumstances to most preserved engines.*

Above: *The same engine, Aveling & Porter 10510, as it was when pictured in May 1992, stripped of everything moveable, in a playground at Stamford, Lincs. Many steam rollers were similarly 'parked up' as children's playthings when they were deemed no longer a viable workhorse. In recent years their increasing value has resulted in most of them being acquired by preservationists and restored to rally condition. A few, however, like 10510, still stand somewhat forlorn, saved from scrap but denied the glory bestowed upon many of their former stablemates.*

Above: *Pictured in the yard of its final commercial owner, near Bidford-on-Avon, in 1960 is Fowler single cylinder ploughing engine 4223, a veteran of 1884. Though not in preservation it was happily to survive the passing of time. It is unusual in that as well as the standard rope winding drum fitted beneath the boiler, it also has a vertical drum affixed to the boiler's side, behind the running board. The encased cylinder block and Salter safety valves are typical early design features. New to J & H Tovey, Cirencester, Glos (paired with Fowler 3896) it later passed to Bomford & Evershed, Salford Priors, Worcs, who operated several sets of steam ploughing tackle.*

Right: *A particularly fine study of an engine designed for rolling tarmac at work at Saxmundham, Suffolk, in 1957. At this time, Wallis & Steevens 'Advance' roller 7920 was still gainfully employed by East Suffolk County Council, being No. 10 in their fleet. The driver can be seen operating the wheel type regulator which governs the amount of steam entering the double high pressure cylinders. The many interesting design features of this modern steam roller are clearly visible, including the absence of a flywheel for quick reversing. A spark arrester is fitted to the chimney to trap any hot emissions and so lessen the risk of fire. This roller has survived the passing of time and is preserved in Yorkshire.*

Above: *At rest by the roadside whilst her crew check essential maintenance points, Aveling & Porter roller 5163 of 1903 releases steam from her safety valves prior to proceeding on her way. This typical example of a 10-ton single cylinder design was used in large numbers to maintain the roads during steam's heyday. This one was new to Billesdon Rural District Council, Leics, later becoming absorbed into the fleet of Leicestershire County Council. It has been in this county all its life and is pictured in May 1965, not far from its home at Cadeby, with a trailer typical of the preservation era in tow.*

Left: *Foden of Sandbach, Cheshire, was this country's most prolific builder of the overtype (locomotive type boilered) steam waggon. The example illustrated, 13488 of 1929, is a later example of the firm's C-type, being fitted with pneumatic-tyred wheels. It also features Ackerman (lorry-type) steering as opposed to the chain-steering of earlier designs. New to Sun Flour Mills, Bromley-by-Bow, London, it saw several ownerships, among them Taroads Ltd of Hatfield, Herts, during which time it carried a tar tank body. It is pictured at Madeira Drive, Brighton, in May 1976, having just successfully completed the Historic Commercial Vehicle Society's annual London to Brighton Run, a distance in excess of 50 miles.*

Few engines can claim to have remained in the same ownership throughout their entire existence. Fowler Class B4 traction engine 7788, however, can boast such a distinction. Purchased from the Steam Plough Works at Leeds in 1897 by the firm of T T Boughton & Sons Ltd of Amersham, Bucks, "Black Jack", as the engine has been named since new, spent all of its working life with this company. Following a lengthy retirement the engine was completely rebuilt and regularly presented at weekend events by them, being pictured at a show at Booker in 1973.

Seen also participating in the HCVS London to Brighton Run, this time in 1989, is Foden C-type wagon 11208, an earlier 1924 example on solid rubber tyred wheels. It had made the long journey from Cornwall to take part and is pictured travelling through Streatham, South London. An end tipper, it spent its entire life working for the Somerset quarry owners, W J King & Sons of Bishops Lydeard, near Taunton, and restored from a derelict hulk over a 10-year period.

Above: *Wallis & Steevens engines appear to have been well favoured by titled gentlemen! 7769, illustrated, a single cylinder traction engine of 1923 was purchased new by Sir Bernard Greenwell, Morden Park, Surrey. "Councillor", as the engine was then named, is seen parading at Hadlow Down, Sussex in 1970. Hanging vertically below the boiler is a set of 'spuds', metal extensions which were bolted to the rear wheels when the engine found itself in difficulty traversing soft ground, the spuds giving the wheels extra grip.*

Right: *Wallis & Steevens of Basingstoke built a wide range of steam vehicles, one of the most popular being their single cylinder traction engine fitted with an 'expansion' valve which made more economic use of the steam. Illustrated is 7625, a 1920 example which began its life with Sir William Cook of Hampstead Norris, Berks. When used commercially, most engines were fitted with steel shod wheels. During preservation, rubber tyres are often added as these make for more comfortable travelling on modern road surfaces. 7625 is pictured at Horsham in 1971.*

Above: *Back in 1907, the RAC was largely responsible for organising a set of trials which set out to demonstrate the advantages of mechanical haulage over horse power. The route took the participating vehicles, both steam and internal combustion, over a varied terrain throughout the roads of England. The overall winner was to be awarded a gold medal. Burrells of Thetford became that overall winner with their 5-ton steam tractor, the design thereafter being branded 'Gold Medal' Tractor. Illustrated at Hadlow Down, Sussex, in May 1970 is 3851, a 1920 example, at the time still in course of restoration. Part of its working life was spent in the ownership of Surrey County Council.*

Left: *Some engines were designed to work in more than one form, Tasker 1409 being an example of a 'convertible' as these were classed. They could either work as a roller, as illustrated, or as a light haulage tractor, when the front roll and headstock would be unbolted at the smokebox bracket and a set of front wheels, perch bracket and axle substituted. Similarly, the rear rolls would be replaced by a set of straked wheels. The example illustrated, at Horsham in 1970, was new as a tractor in 1909, returning to the makers' works at Andover in 1930 and rebuilt as a roller, in which form it has since remained. It is fitted with an unusual 5-section front roll.*

Right: *The firm of Babcock & Wilcox Ltd, better known for their water-tube boiler plants, marketed only a handful of rollers that they had inherited upon taking over Clayton & Shuttleworth in 1924. These were essentially the same design as the Clayton machines and just five exist in preservation, of which 95/4009 of 1926 is a 6-ton single cylinder example. All survivors went new to Somerset road rolling contractors, W W Buncombe Ltd of Highbridge, who fitted the distinctive style of half canopy. From work, 95/4009 went into preservation in Kent and is pictured at Horsham in 1970.*

Below: *A group of engines prepare to make their way to the arena for the grand parade at Horsham in 1971. To the left can be seen Tasker convertible roller 1409 of 1909, Burrell 'Gold Medal' tractor 3851 saunters in at the rear and to the fore is Wallis & Steevens 'Advance' roller 7972 of 1928. The latter engine is one of the most up to date examples of a steam roller being designed to cope with the new tarmacadam road surfaces of the day. One attribute was instant reversal which avoided creating ridges in the soft tarmac, plus even weight distribution fore and aft, pannier tanks replacing the more traditional rear water tank.*

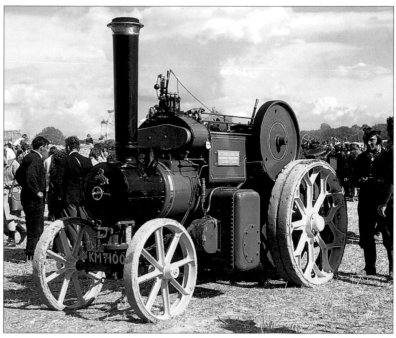

Above: *Although best known for the road rollers that they built in large numbers, the firm of Aveling & Porter of Rochester, Kent, also marketed various other types of steam vehicle, including a range of 5-ton tractors, among them the Class L, a compound design fitted with piston valves, of which 11486 is an example. It was one of a number operated by Kent County Council being supplied in 1925 as their fleet No. 35. A number of this type were later rebuilt in roller form in order to prolong their working life. "Morning Star" has been rallied for many years in various ownerships and is pictured at Horsham in 1972.*

Left: *The firm of Ransomes Sims & Jefferies of Ipswich, Suffolk, were responsible for designing and building a wide range of agricultural equipment, including some extremely well-built traction engines, their 6nhp compound design having very pleasing lines. No. 41046 is a late example, built in 1930 and new to R F Fenn, Frating, Essex, who also owned another similar engine (35247). Interesting features are the inclined pump for replenishing water in the boiler and the buffing pads on the boiler sides which prevent the front wheels from creating dents in the boiler cladding when on full lock. The engine is pictured at Horsham in 1970.*

Above: *There is always something special about steaming an engine along the highway, though it requires a lot of concentration and a well-seasoned crew in today's modern traffic. Burrell single cylinder traction engine 4048 "William the Second" is pictured proceeding at leisure along the A272 near Petersfield, Hants in June 1970. These days, many engines are ferried to and from events by transporter but each summer a number of organised road runs are staged by preservation groups, thus allowing a variety of engines to be seen in their proper environment, often with authentic loads in tow.*

Right: *A neat little 6-ton Fowler single cylinder roller 19032 which has had a very interesting working life, having travelled around the world and back. New in 1932, she was one of a number exported to the Dutch East Indies, the pressure gauge being graduated in "atmospheres" rather than the usual "lbs per square inch". She later returned to this country to become part of the fleet of the Mechanical Tar Spraying & Grouting Co Ltd of Reading, Berks. Eventually finding a preservation owner in Sussex, she is pictured at the Horsham Rally in September 1970.*

Above: *Two interesting comparisons in design of Burrell showman's road locomotive at Crystal Palace in September 1959. To the left can be seen 3489 "King George VI", a 1913 example rated at 6nhp which began its life as a road haulage engine in Devon, being rebuilt in its present form some years later for London and Home Counties showman, Swales Bolesworth of Dagenham. It has the distinction of being the first showman's engine to attend a traction engine rally. To the right is 3887 "The Prince of Wales", a larger, 8nhp example, built in 1922 for Wiltshire showman, Henry Jennings of Devizes, to haul and power his Whale Scenic Railway, one of the "hi-tech" thrill rides of the day!*

Left: *Most manufacturers gave their 5-ton steam tractors a distinctive design name. Fosters of Lincoln called theirs the 'Wellington' tractor and the example illustrated, 14514 of 1925, sports a fine painting of the Duke of Wellington on its pannier tank. It spent its life on haulage work for the Moel Faen Slate Quarry, Denbigh and has seen a number of owners in preservation. When exhibited at the Horsham Rally in 1972, it was resident in the London area and spent a number of years as an exhibit at the Kew Bridge Steam Museum where one of the authors sometimes drove her.*

Right: *Following the grand parade at a steam rally, the engines often line up in the arena for a photocall. Among those participating at Horsham in 1970 are, from the right: Ruston Proctor single cylinder traction engine 36828, a 1909 example which spent its working life in Kent; a smaller example of a general purpose engine by William Foster, 14638, built much later in 1933 and which has the unusual (for this class of engine) addition of belly tanks for extra water capacity; and the Burrell showman's road locomotives 3443 "Lord Nelson" and 3887 "The Prince of Wales". Seeing several different engines in line abreast clearly illustrates the design features of the various types.*

Left: *Royalty on parade! Burrell showman's road locomotive 3443 "Lord Nelson" heads 3887 "The Prince of Wales" during the grand parade at Horsham Rally in 1970. 3443 spent much of her working life on the westcountry fairgrounds with amusement caterers, Anderton & Rowland, being supplied to them in 1913. A later showland owner was John Cole of Bristol and the engine has seen a number of preservation owners, including the National Motor Museum at Beaulieu.*

Above: *A number of heavy haulage engines were supplied with a front crane (detachable when not required), enabling loads to be lifted by the engine as well as being transported. Burrell 3829 was new in 1920 to T & W F Hooper of Liskeard, Cornwall, but within a few months had been sold to the well-known London engineering and haulage company, J Hickey & Sons of Richmond, being afforded the name "His Majesty" which it has carried through to preservation. The drive shaft used to operate the crane's worm geared lifting drum can be clearly seen in this study taken at Horsham in 1970.*

Left: *Wallis & Steevens were responsible for a number of interesting steam roller designs. Their standard three-point machine (one roll at the front and two at the rear) is well illustrated in 7779, a 10-ton example of 1923 which was built to the order of E Parry & Co, Putney, London, later passing to the well-known firm of contractors, A J Ward & Sons, Egham, Surrey. The firm finished many of their rollers in brown livery and several are preserved in varying shades of the colour. Pictured at Horsham in 1970, the makers' distinctive style of headstock will be noted.*

41

Looking rather sorry for itself as it stands apparently abandoned at the roadside near St Columb, Cornwall, in September 1962, is McLaren ploughing engine 1552. In fact, the 1918-built engine had recently arrived in the area, having been purchased for preservation from a market gardener in Somerset who had used it to supply steam for the sterilisation of greenhouse soil. Before this, "Hero" had been used along with its partner engine (unfortunately no longer with us) to cultivate the land in various counties from Northamptonshire to Gloucestershire. The engine is still resident in the Duchy of Cornwall and is the sole known survivor of its size.

A further example of a steam roller at work, this time a 10-ton Marshall single 77474 of 1924. Built at Gainsborough, Lincs, this example was supplied new to John Ball & Sons of Forton, Lancs, but later joined the fleet of R Dingle & Sons Ltd, Stoke Climsland, Cornwall, who at the time operated a very large fleet of steam rollers. 77474 is pictured rolling hardcore in this firm's ownership in May 1960, at Landrake in East Cornwall. The paintwork is well-seasoned and the top of the front headstock has been removed, possibly for routine maintenance. A handwheel visible behind the rear roll operated a scarifier, a fitment comprising a pair of tines which could be used to rip up an old road surface. The roller is now preserved in Cornwall.

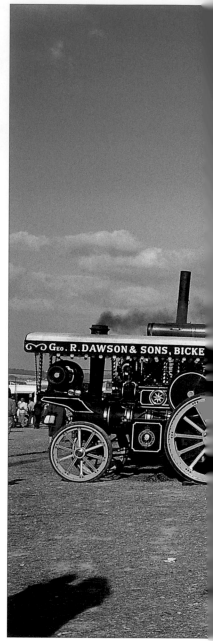

This galloping horse roundabout, or set of 'gallopers',
is shown at the one and only Shottesbrooke Steam
Fair, Berkshire, in 1964. The best surviving examples
of old machines were presented by invitation, with
preserved showman's engines driving the lights, in the
grounds of a country house. It was never repeated but
its popularity led to the description 'steam fair' being
used for lesser events. This set of gallopers was built
in 1900 at a time when such machines were among
the most popular on the fairground. The coming of
faster machines and the depression of the 1930s caused
many of them to be destroyed, but today they are
much sought after and several are in preservation.
This one survived the lean years to be bought by the
Noyce family in Hampshire in about 1950. It was
then rebuilt. The steam centre engine was sold into
preservation and replaced by electric drive while the
paintwork, lighting and road transport were restored
to exemplary condition. The machine travels widely
and has probably paid for itself many times over.

Steam and the fairground: the scene creates a certain nostalgia that attracts both young and old. Where better to savour the experience than at the Great Dorset Steam Fair, held annually at Tarrant Hinton, near Blandford Forum on the Wednesday to Sunday following the Late Summer Bank Holiday. A line of showman's engines generating and powering the rides stretches almost to infinity, recreating a scene of yesteryear for all to enjoy. Our scene is taken at the 1989 event. The engine nearest the camera is Foster showman's tractor 14066 "Endeavour" which worked the fairgrounds with John Beach of Sunbury, Middx. The rides form a magnificent selection which graced the tobers of yesteryear: lighthouse slip, galloping horses, switchback, big wheel and steam yachts (swings).

A number of other steam shows also offer a respectable line-up of showman-type engines at their annual presentation. Pictured at St Agnes, Cornwall, in August 1990, from the left, are: Burrells 3949 "Princess Mary" (1922), 2072 "The Masterpiece" (1898), 3849 "Princess Marina" (1920), Garrett 32122 "The Greyhound" (1914) and Fowler 17290 "Jubilee" (1927). The last-mentioned is a preservation conversion from a roller, representing a practice that is not to everyone's liking.

Fowler were the foremost builders of ploughing engines, their Leeds factory being named The Steam Plough Works. The most popular class of this engine was the 16nhp BB1 of which 15163 is an example. New in 1918 to G Gunter of Wetherby, North Yorks, it ended its days working in Cambridgeshire, from where it was acquired for preservation in 1970. It has been rebuilt as a 'working' engine and looks just as it might have done when earning its living. Our picture, taken at St Issey, Cornwall, in 1990, shows it during the evening sunshine, every bit the well oiled workhorse. The rope winding drum, used to haul the tackle, can clearly be seen. The hosepipe is used for drawing water when the rear tank needs replenishing.

Very few ploughing engines are used commercially today. One exception is a pair of Fowler Class AA7s (18nhp) 15364 and 15365, named "Windsor" and "Sandringham", which are used for the cable dredging of lakes several times a year. Although they have visited the occasional rally, they are not officially preserved but true working engines. No. 15364 is pictured near Helston, Cornwall, in May 1997, where it was in use with its partner engine dredging a lake on an estate. Not for this one the spick and span magnificence of a rally-going engine! The wire rope to the dredge is extended to the right of the picture, whilst the rope attached to the front perch bracket forms an anchor to help resist engine movement during the strain of the pull.

Only one pair of Burrell ploughing engines is known to survive, 776 & 777, which date from 1879. The former is pictured at Weeting, Norfolk, in 1987. Quite a small example of its type, rated at 8nhp, it began its working career with R G W Wilberforce of Woolavington and was rescued for preservation from a scrapyard in very rough condition in the 1960s. This class of engine worked in pairs, one positioned each side of a field, and the implement used to cultivate the land was drawn between them using a wire rope extended from the drum mounted beneath the boiler. Early design features are evident on 776, notably the Salter safety valves on the cylinder block and the square pattern riveted tender. Later designs incorporated flanging which withstood the rigours of wear and tear (particularly rusting) for much longer.

Brown & May of Devizes were a small engineering company in comparison with some steam engine manufacturers, building mainly portable engines. An exception is their sole-surviving example of a showman's road locomotive "General Buller", No. 8742, built in 1912 and which spent much of its showland life with Hibble & Mellors of Nottingham. The dynamo and smokebox extension were later removed when the engine was relegated to agricultural duties, but restoration to its former glory has since taken place, as this picture, taken at the Great Dorset Steam Fair in 1987, illustrates.

A popular post-World War I design of Aveling & Porter roller was the E-type, a 10-tonner with a single cylinder and piston valve. No 10159 of 1921 spent her working life in Essex, Berks and Bucks. She is seen here in about 1985 under the gantry outside the Kew Bridge Steam Museum in West London for attention to the gears. Beneath the rear-mounted toolbox carrying the registration number can be seen the lid of the water filler for the tender and the full-width towing hitch. Leaning up against the offside roll are the fire irons which an engine always carries. This roller belonged to one of the authors for 26 years, having been bought in 1968 after lying derelict in the yard of T T Boughton of Amersham for 15 years. Restoration to working order was done in the open but full repainting was not carried out. She was displayed in typical working trim, at first in Bucks and later in south-west London and Surrey, always travelling under steam. She moved to Cornwall when her owner retired in 1988.

Above: *No. 10159 seen again, this time in 1995 at Camborne's Trevithick Day in Cornwall. Now in the ownership of local enthusiast Graham Viant, the engine has been completely repainted and lined out in what is believed to be the makers' original livery, traces of which had been kept. Author and previous owner Kenneth Brown is on the footplate and co-author Alan Thomas is behind the camera.*

The engine is coupled to a home-made water cart in readiness for a long day out. While standing at Boughtons in the 1950s and 60s, a vigorous blackberry bush grew up through the gear casing. This, plus the fact that the firm's traction engine "Black Jack" (illustrated on page 24) was standing nearby, gave rise to the name "Blackberry Jack" which the engine now carries.

Right: *An earlier example of an Aveling & Porter 5-ton tractor is 6093 of 1906, being of the XAC class. New to Kent haulage contractors, Busbridge & Co Ltd of East Malling, she remained in that county in various ownerships throughout her working life. She was acquired for preservation by pioneer enthusiast, Don Eastwood of Horsmonden, in whose ownership she is pictured at Paddock Wood in 1957, rejoicing in the name "Bert". The brass prancing horse mounted on the smokebox door (the steed of Odin) and 'Invicta' scroll, are a feature on all Aveling products.*

Left: *This 8-ton Aveling & Porter roller No 11698 is seen in Sri Lanka in 1983. Though not obvious from the photograph, the strapped-up headstock has started to tear away from the badly-corroded smokebox and the roller has simply been pushed into the bush by the roadside. Otherwise she seemed in fair condition and had clearly been working almost to the time she was spotted. Indeed, her driver appeared from nowhere within seconds of the camera being produced! This roller was one of a batch supplied to Ceylon in 1927 with only a single speed for simplicity of operation. Today engines such as this are being repatriated to the UK to satisfy the continuing demand for examples suitable for preservation.*

Below: *Most steam engine builders had a strong export market, with large numbers being sent to countries like South Africa and Australia. Such an engine was Burrell 10nhp compound traction 3130 which went new to New Zealand in 1909 and which recently returned to Great Britain for a three year 'steam tour' before going back home again. Strange as it might seem for such a big engine, it was originally used for direct ploughing but more extensively for haulage and threshing. The exceptionally long boiler is of note, also the belly tanks, normally only found on road locomotives in this country. The large lamp attached in front of the chimney is a typical New Zealand feature. The engine is pictured at Weeting in July 1996.*

A pleasing view of a portable engine on the belt to a set of threshing tackle at Bishops Castle in 1982. The engine is Edward Humphries No. 1663, built at Pershore, Worcs. in 1886. Portable engines were originally hauled by a team of horses, and having arrived at a farm with the engine in readiness for the job in hand, they had to return to their starting point to collect the threshing tackle before the toil could commence. The handle attached to the firebox is the regulator which, when turned, altered the speed at which the engine worked by controlling the flow of steam. The pressure gauge is mounted directly above. The tall chimney extension would be lowered when the engine was moved to its next place of work.

Another small engineering firm which built only a few engines was Gibbons & Robinson of Wantage, Berks. (now Oxon). The only example to survive the passage of time is No. 959 of 1891, which was purchased new by Thomas Swain, Warrington, Lancs. It was rebuilt later in its working life when it acquired the cylinders and motion of a later Wantage engine (No. 1432) and is currently preserved in Herefordshire, being pictured at Much Marcle in 1992. The red painted cross-arm governor, which ensured that the engine worked at optimum speed whilst on the belt, can be seen in this view.

Below: *The final version of the company to build engines at Wantage was the Wantage Engineering Co Ltd. Only two examples from this era survive, both being single cylinder traction engines, one built in 1900 (1389) and this 1908 example, 1522 "Pioneer", which is pictured at Sellindge, Kent in 1976. New to an Oxfordshire owner, it ended its days in a Swindon scrapyard, being rescued and restored by a Kentish enthusiast during the 1970s. Following several changes of ownership in that area, it was sold to an enthusiast in Ireland during 1996.*

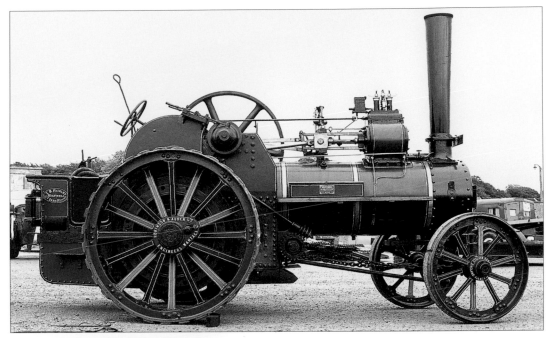

Above: *Gibbons & Robinson later reformed to become Robinson & Auden and as with its predecessors, just one traction engine has survived, this being 1376 of 1900 which was new to the Hulke Colliery Co, Lydney, Glos.*
The design has changed little in the space of ten years. The rectangular fitting next to the safety valves is a mechanical lubricator which ensures that the cylinder is adequately supplied with oil.
Preserved in North Yorkshire, the engine is pictured at Lanark in Scotland during June 1982.

*Aveling-Barford Ltd of Grantham is a name
long associated with road making equipment.
The firm began producing steam rollers in the
1930s, following the demise of Aveling &
Porter of Rochester. Their rollers were designed
to be as simple as possible for export to the
Third World. However, they are a delight to
drive and a number found buyers in the UK,
one of which was AG785 of 1946, an 8-ton
single cylinder purchased new by Tipton
Corporation, Staffs. Notable features on this
late design were water ballast rolls (to enable
the weight to be increased if necessary), side
mounted coal bunkers with footplate access
between and spartan galvanised canopy. AG785
is pictured at an event at Booker in 1973.*

An authentically restored Foden waggon pictured in correct period livery at Horsham in 1972. 10788 was in fact never owned commercially by Tate & Lyle Ltd, but as none of their own waggons have survived the passing of time, this 6-ton C-type was acquired and restored by the company. It was new in 1922 to James Shipton & Sons Ltd, New Basford, Notts, being traded in by the makers in 1929 and rebuilt for Hunters Ltd of Ardwick, Manchester. The chain-drive to the rear axle can be seen, also the water tank mounted between the frames. The waggon is currently on display at the British Commercial Vehicle Museum at Leyland, Lancs.

Above: *As well as steam waggons, Fodens also produced a range of haulage tractors, of which their D-type was the most popular. Basically a shortened version of their waggon, with larger rear wheels, it was designed to haul one or two trucks. The canopy was extended at the back to cover the coal bunker which was hopper fed into the cab. The water tank is mounted beneath the bunker. The first owner of "Perseverance" when new in 1928 was A L Watkins, Crickhowell, Brecon and during World War II it was employed by London County Council to assist with demolition work during the blitz. An early preservation piece, it is pictured at Crystal Palace in 1959.*

Right: *Emitting a staccato exhaust as it flies full flight through Purley on the occasion of the 1974 HCVS Run is Super Sentinel waggon 5407 which started life in 1924 with J B Kind of Burton-upon-Trent. It eventually ended up as part of the extensive fleet of the United Africa Co Ltd of Liverpool, who operated Sentinel waggons until the early 1960s, hence several have survived to be preserved. This particular waggon is notable in having travelled 'end to end' from John O'Groats to Lands End, one of a number to complete the journey successfully back in the summer of 1976.*

Super Sentinel 6504 began life in 1926 in waggon form with Vick Bros of Aldershot. On finishing its working life, it was sold to a Surrey scrap merchant who cut it in half through the chassis. When acquired for preservation, it was restored with shortened chassis as a tractor (based on Sentinel's own design). Many such vehicles operated in the 1930s when they were similarly converted following crippling taxation applied to steam waggons in favour of the rising stars of the day, the internal combustion engined lorries. 6504 is pictured at Streatham Hill during the 1980 London to Brighton Run, towing a period trailer suitably loaded. The chain-drive to the rear axle is clearly depicted.

The Sentinel S-type series was the
final development of the
company's steam waggon to be
sold on the home market and was
available in 4, 6 and 8-wheel
format. The design was extremely
up to date for a steam vehicle. A
vertical boiler and undertype
engine were still incorporated but
the chain drive of earlier models
was replaced by shaft drive,
enabling the waggon to be capable
of speeds of up to 50mph!
Illustrated at Egham, Surrey, in
1991 is No. 8821, an S6 3-way
tipper which was new to Tarmac
Ltd of Wolverhampton in 1933,
now handsomely preserved in its
original livery.

Above: *The design of the Sentinel S-type waggon allows considerable scope for the authentic application of period liveries. No. 9016, illustrated, an S4 of 1934, was new to coal merchants and contractors, E&A Shadrack Ltd of East Ham, London, and has been superbly restored to original appearance, even to the extent of the trailer, finished in matching livery. The outfit features deep sided bodywork to increase the payload. Note the safety chain running from the trailer to the rear of the waggon which was regular practice with steam vehicles. The picture was taken at Walcot Hall, Shropshire, in August 1993.*

Right: *The Yorkshire Patent Steam Wagon Co. of Leeds produced a range of waggons which were quite unlike the designs of most other companies. They used a transverse boiler with undertype engine, early examples having chain-drive to the rear axle. The external appearance changed over the years but the basic design of boiler remained the same. No. 117 is the oldest survivor of this firm's products, being new in 1905 to the Hon. J C Best of Llangollen. No cab was fitted, leaving the crew totally exposed to the elements. The waggon had wooden wheels fitted with steel tyres, and a rear mounted water tank. Our picture shows "Pendle Maid" at Bicton Arena, Devon, in 1982.*

Above: *Present day rallies often organise their steam section around a particular theme. The Carrington event, held annually during the Spring Bank Holiday Weekend, in 1994 featured an impressive entry of portable engines. Their extreme simplicity is evident. Nearest the camera are two Tuxfords, 1131 and 1238 of 1883 and 1887, respectively. These little engines were built locally at Boston. A quartet of Marshalls stand next in line. The maroon painted example is fitted with the maker's distinctive 'Britannia' circular type firebox and is a late design being built in 1935. Portable engines continued to be manufactured by some companies, mainly for export to the Third World, well into the 1950s.*

Right: *As well as a break from the traditional with their 'Advance' steam roller for tarmac work, Wallis & Steevens produced a very unusual, compact 3-ton design which they designated their 'Simplicity' type. To the uninitiated, it may look far from simple with its strange, angled boiler but it was purported to be a relatively easy roller to drive and one which needed a minimum of maintenance. The water tank is carried beneath the boiler with the coal bunkers mounted on its sloping edge. Steering is by worm and sector. The absence of a rear tank and tender allowed easy footplate access. No. 7832, illustrated, was the prototype and was new in 1926 to E Parry & Co of Putney, London. It is pictured at Stonehouse, Glos, in September 1984.*

Above: *A number of engines were built as semi-portables, the wheels being removed on arrival at the work site and then remaining static. Robey 49116 is particularly interesting as it is also an 'undertype' design, with the cylinder and motion carried beneath the boiler. A large pulley is mounted on the crankshaft end and the flywheel (not in camera) is fitted to the offside. A huge safety valve is mounted on top of the firebox and a large manhole (for boiler inspection purposes and for washing out) is fitted to the side of the boiler. The complete engine is now mounted on a trolley for ease of movement. It spent its working days in a Northumberland sawmill and is pictured at the Great Dorset Steam Fair in 1995.*

Left: *Robey & Co were one of several firms to have their factory at Lincoln, building many types of engine, among them a neat 6nhp single cylinder agricultural of 8.5-tons weight. This broadside view shows No. 42675 of 1927 on parade at Elvaston Castle, Derby, in 1987. A Pickering governor is fitted and also visible is the ashpan damper. This device is used to open or close the lid of the ashpan in order to increase or decrease the amount of draught to the underside of the fire, particularly useful when raising steam. This engine spent most of its working life in Leicestershire and is preserved in North Lincs.*

J & H McLaren of Leeds made what might almost be called the 'Rolls-Royce' of traction engines, in quality of engineering if not in embellishment. No 547 of 1894 worked for nearly 50 years on the firm's estates in Northants. Her rugged good looks attracted the attention of the late Charles Gregory (credited with having started the preservation movement in Cornwall) whilst on a tour of engines in Oxfordshire in 1958. He bought her, but not wishing to incur the cost of a low-loader from Great Tew to Camborne, decided to steam her the 251 miles with the help of his elder daughter and a friend. The trip took just eleven days, not only creating a record for an unsprung engine but the faultless performance after several years under a sheet was a great tribute to her builders. When photographed at St Agnes in 1991, she had passed to Fred and Olive Britton of Tiverton, Devon, who were still keeping her in working trim with unlined black paintwork. One of the authors can testify to the ease with which one man can handle her on the road.

The 6nhp single cylinder traction engine built
by Marshall of Gainsborough was one of the
most popular of agricultural engines, being a
handy size for travelling the narrow roads and
easily manoeuvrable in confined areas such as
stackyards. Looking just as it might have done
on leaving the Britannia Ironworks, No. 45689
of 1906 is seen parading at Carrington, Lincs,
in May 1992. The maroon livery, correctly lined
out, and the black painted flywheel are
according to manufacturer's specification. New
to T Jackson of Arnold, Hull, East Yorks,
"Dorothy" has been a part of the rally scene
since the 1950s.

actors we.

to R J

Some lighter engines could be used quite successfully for direct ploughing as they did not compress the ground too much in front of the plough. An example is this steam tractor built by the Mann Patent Steam Cart & Wagon Co of Leeds. Seen giving a demonstration at a ploughing match at Seale, Surrey, in 1981 is Mann 1260, built in 1917. The engine is designed to be operable by one person, with side-mounted coal bunker and water cart to the rear. The unusual design of the wheels is noteworthy. These tractors were also used for light haulage, this particular example being supplied new to J Clarke of Sampford, Essex.

J & F Howard of Bedford produced a number of oddball engines, some of which were adapted for ploughing. No. 201, pictured at Manby, Lincs, in 1990, was built in 1872 and was sent new to Australia, being repatriated in the 1980s. The cylinder is mounted in the tender and its end can just be seen at the top right hand side. The flywheel is carried in a much lower position to align with the crankshaft. The blast pipe which carries the exhaust steam through to the chimney is carried under the boiler. There are only two Howard engines in preservation, the other also having recently returned to England following many years on display at the Henry Ford Museum in the USA.

Yet another engine to be repatriated from Australia in recent times. Marshall road locomotive 52962 was exported new in 1909 via the firm's agents, R C Scrutton & Co Ltd of Sydney. The present owner purchased the engine without even having seen it, after it was advertised in the preservation press and has restored it to the fine condition as pictured at the Great Dorset Steam Fair in 1992. Although several examples of this large Marshall product were exported, few were sold on the home market, so it is interesting to see one returning to its country of origin in preservation.

Steam fire engines are not as often seen at rallies as other classes of engine, though a number have been preserved. In reality a special type of portable engine, Merryweather 2541 is a very rare example, believed built at the firm's Greenwich works in the 1870s and one of just two known to exist with horizontal cylinders and pump action. It was for many years on a private estate near Camborne, Cornwall, and is now preserved by the West of England Steam Engine Society who are in the process of restoring it to working order. Steam fire engines were horse-drawn, the driver sitting up front with up to four crew members sitting on the platform behind. The fireman would stand on a footplate at the rear (removed in the photograph) to ensure that steam was up by the time the fire was reached. The rear platform also carried the coal bunkers and the hoses would be strapped to the engine's sides. Pictured at St Issey, Cornwall, in 1995.

Left: *Tasker of Andover marketed two designs of steam tractor, one gear-driven and the other with chain drive to the rear axle. An example of the latter is No. 1741 of 1917, new to Albert Aylett, East Dean, Sussex. The chain is hidden beneath the curved casing seen above the hind wheel. The chain-drives were fast little machines, speeds of 20mph being not uncommon. Tasker tractors were designated 'The Little Giant' and were used mainly for light haulage. 1741 is pictured at Rushmoor Rally, near Aldershot in 1989 in the ownership of the Hardwick family, well-known scrap merchants, who were also instrumental in saving many engines from the cutter's torch.*

Below: *Not only have a number of British-built engines returned to their homeland in recent years but also some more unusual examples built by foreign manufacturers. Zettelmeyer 553 is a 10-ton roller built in Germany in 1930 and spent its working life in France from where it was purchased by its present owner in 1971. The layout is basically similar to a British-built machine but the cast rolls are decidedly different, as is the piston valve cylinder block and motion. The driver has one hand on the regulator, which governs the engine's speed, and the other on the reversing lever, used to determine the direction in which the engine is travelling, and also, when necessary, to call it to a halt. The scene is depicted at Quex Park, Kent, in 1983.*

An engine which has twice seen extensive restoration is Clayton & Shuttleworth compound traction engine 48279 of 1919. Following exhibition at the Royal Show, she was sold to the Swimbridge Steam Threshing Co in Devon and worked in that county all her life. When retired, she lay abandoned at the bottom of a field, often partly submerged in water in winter. Over the years, practically all of her boiler fittings were robbed and when acquired for restoration in the 1960s, she was a derelict hulk, so badly deteriorated that no fewer than three prospective preservationists gave up on her. The present owner, however, decided that she was worth the untold perseverance required to bring her back from the dead and "Phoenix", as she has been named, is indeed an engine which has risen from the ashes.

Occasionally, an engine is taken to a rally in part-restored condition, in order that the general public might gain an insight into the amount of work required to create a gleaming preservation piece. Clayton & Shuttleworth single cylinder traction engine 36731 "Old Glory" of 1904, is pictured at Duncombe Park, Yorkshire, in 1993. All major boiler work has been completed, which includes a new firebox, boiler barrel, smokebox, boiler tubes and tender. The cylinder block has obviously seen considerable attention and the front wheels and perch have been shot-blasted and primed. At the time, there was still much to do before the engine moved under its own power, but with firebox stayheads shining in the morning sunshine, it reflects great credit on its owner.

Above: *Some engines have been in deplorable condition when rescued for preservation. A typical example is 1925 Foden C-type waggon 11850 which was one of several purchased new by Somerset quarry owners, W J King & Sons of Bishops Lydeard, near Taunton. When pensioned off in the early 1930s, it lay discarded at the rear of the firm's yard for more than 50 years, gradually deteriorating until it became almost unrecognisable. The chimney had broken off, the cab completely rotted away and the remains of the tipping body lying upside down alongside. Few thought that it could be rebuilt to its former glory when it came under the hammer in May 1988 but the majority were to be proved wrong!*

Right: *Can this be the same engine pictured as a derelict hulk? Indeed it is. Foden 11850, proudly displaying its original name "Superior", ascends with ease the long climb towards Pease Pottage as it participates in the 1995 HCVS London to Brighton Run. Though carrying its original owner's livery, this outstanding job of restoration is attributed to owner Colin Waite and his willing band of helpers. The waggon is virtually a new machine, with a complete new boiler and bodywork. It illustrates just what can be achieved with the required ability and dedication.*

Above: *With today's demand for engines and the steam engineering facilities now available, very few derelict wrecks are considered beyond restoration. But this one is! It is an early Clayton & Shuttleworth duplex cylindered portable engine (18602 of 1880) that was found accidentally by an excavator driver in Cornwall's china clay country. He was using his machine to remove an old waste tip on the edge of a pit when his bucket struck what he thought was a rock. The destruction of the engine that ensued, nearly every casting being smashed, is clearly evident. Fragments of spur gearing and a winding drum indicate that the engine had been used for hoisting sand waste material and had simply been buried in the tip when its services were no longer required.*

Right: *Garrett's '4CD' model was the most popular of all the nominal 5-ton steam tractors, with many surviving the passing of time. No. 35225 is reputed to be the last example to have been built, in September 1929. Its first owner was C Light & Co Ltd, Christchurch, Hants, but much of its time has been spent in the North of England. Originally it would have been fitted with motion covers but these have been removed during preservation. Currently based near York, it is pictured at the Pickering Rally in July 1993.*

Above: *A nice portrayal of a steam roller 'road train'. Garrett compound roller 34084 approaches Saxtead Green, Suffolk, whilst participating in the Three Counties Steam Tour during May 1997. The roller was new to East Suffolk County Council and was revisiting its old stamping ground from its present base in Cheshire. During the run, it called at its birthplace, the former Garrett factory, now the Longshop Museum, at Leiston, Suffolk. With living van and water cart in tow, it recreates a typical scene of yesteryear as a roller moved to its next work site.*

Left: *One of the more unusual products to emerge from the Sandbach works of Foden was the 'Sun' tractor of which No. 13630 is an example. This little engine used the same type of boiler and motion as was fitted to the firm's Speed 6 and Speed 12 undertype waggons and is quite a speedy little machine on the road although bouncy on its springs. This particular example was exported new in 1930 to South Africa, where it was used for direct ploughing work. It returned to these shores in the 1980s and is now preserved in Cornwall, where the picture was taken in June 1992. The driver's position can be clearly seen. The coal bunker is to the left of the driver's seat and the water tank underneath. It is one of just two examples known to exist.*

Fowler adapted some of their rollers to carry out a variety of road-making activities. No. 17506 was one such engine, being supplied to the Mechanical Tar Spraying & Grouting Co Ltd of Reading as a 'Fowler-Wood Complete Roadmaking Machine', specially equipped with front tanks to carry the tar and a pump, which was chain-driven via a sprocket on the flywheel boss, to force the tar through a rear spray bar. With a chipping hopper in tow, it could tar, chip and roll a road. "Undaunted", as this engine is named, is one of the few surviving examples complete with all fittings intact and is pictured on a road run at Sonning Common, Berks, in May 1992.

Wallis & Steevens engines were built at Basingstoke. Their version of the 5-ton tractor was known as the 'Oilbath' design, the crankshaft and motion being enclosed in an oil-tight casing, thus protecting them from the elements and ensuring thorough lubrication. Pannier tanks were fitted instead of the more usual belly tanks. The example illustrated, No. 7289 of 1912, carries a raised bunker for extra coal capacity and was new to D Cobb of Bere Regis, Dorset. It is pictured at Camborne, Cornwall in April 1996, awaiting its transporter following an appearance at the town's Trevithick Day which is held annually on the last Saturday of the month.

The distinct lines of a 'Colonial' engine are evident in this single cylinder Ruston Proctor traction engine 44180 of 1912, which was built as a straw burner and exported to the Philippines. Now back on home ground, it is pictured at the Knowl Hill Rally, near Maidenhead, Berks, in 1993. The flywheel is mounted on the offside, opposite to the conventional, and there are large railed bunkers at the rear for carrying the straw fuel. The raised 'paddles' on the extra wide rear wheels are to assist traction on soft ground.

One or two examples of American-built traction engines have been imported to this country in recent years, among them this Case, thought to be No. C632 of 1907. Its appearance is very different from that of British design. There is no boiler lagging, the flywheel, fitted with a clutch, is mounted on the opposite side, steam is collected in a dome and the cylinder block (in this picture away from the camera) is mounted on the side of the boiler. Access to the footplate is via the rear of the engine and the wheel spokes are narrow and of circular section. These engines worked in teams, threshing on the American prairies, and were fired on the straw accumulated during the day's work. The engine is pictured at Wincanton, Somerset, in August 1992.

Aveling & Porter of Rochester built this unusual tandem roller 7411 in 1911, it being their first attempt at a quick reverse design for working with hot asphalt. The cylinders, built to Ephraim Shay's American patent, are mounted vertically on the offside hornplate with the motion beneath enclosed, as illustrated, and a 100-gallon water tank is similarly mounted on the nearside in an attempt to counterbalance the engine. Only 10 were built, of which this is the prototype and sole survivor. New in 1912 to Fulham Corporation, London, it was sold in 1928 to W W Buncombe Ltd of Highbridge, Somerset who last used it in 1953. Preserved in Berkshire, it is pictured at Rushmoor Rally, near Aldershot in July 1989.

One of three rollers supplied to the Great Western Railway at Paddington just prior to nationalisation in 1948, Aveling-Barford AH162 is believed to be the last Class W (10-ton) example of its make to have been built. She is fitted with water ballast rolls and would originally have carried the standard issue galvanised iron canopy. "Omega" later worked for Joseph Coles & Sons of Bristol before passing into preservation in 1962 when she travelled a distance of 180 miles to her new home in West Cornwall. She is pictured on the road near Redruth in May 1987, with a traditional workman's living van in tow. When rollers worked commercially, this would provide the accommodation for the driver and his family who often spent weeks away from home working on a particular road mending job.

Pictured against a rural backdrop at the Great Dorset Steam Fair in September 1985, Allchin single cylinder traction engine 1173 awaits its duties 'on the belt'. The Northampton-built engine left the Globe Works in 1901 for the ownership of W Vousden, Eastry, Kent, spending the whole of its working life in the Garden of England. Its final owners, before departing for preservation in Dorset, were the Folkstone & District Water Company who bestowed upon it the name "Aquarius". Many of the engine's working components are well documented in this study including the rod from the footplate to the cylinder drain taps. The toolbox mounted beneath the short running board on the boiler side is a typical Allchin feature.

A
CAVALCADE
OF
TRACTION
ENGINES

Fowler 7459 belies her years, being built as long ago as 1895, and clearly illustrates how little the basic traction engine design changed over the years. A Class A4 single cylinder example, rated at 6nhp, "Endurance" was new to Eddison & de Mattos of Dorchester, a firm better known for their ploughing engines and later for their large fleet of steam rollers. She later passed to the Oxford Steam Plough Co of Cowley, eventually ending up in a Berkshire scrapyard, from where she was rescued for preservation in the 1960s. Pictured at the Horsham Rally in 1972, with a threshing demonstration in full swing in the background.

Another view of the unusual Fowler Class E1 steam tractor 11799, rated at 5nhp and weighing 7-tons. New to the War Department in 1909 and used for gun haulage, she was later acquired by Nelson Noyce of Farnborough, Hants, a travelling showman, who rebuilt her for a life on the fairground, mounting a dynamo on the front smokebox extension and lengthening the canopy to cover the instrument. He gave her the name she still carries "The Victory". For many years the engine was owned and rallied by the late Bill Druce of Bognor Regis, being pictured in his ownership at Horsham in 1971. She is seen passing a line of commercial vehicles, another popular sector of the preservation scene.

Ransomes Sims & Jefferies 6nhp compound traction engine 42035 was one of the last to be built by this Ipswich-based company, being completed in 1932 and sold to a Lincolnshire dealer. In 1935, it went to Reynolds Bros of Plumstead, Norfolk, a county where it was to spend the whole of its working life. It was one of the earliest engines to be preserved in Leicestershire and is pictured turning into a yard at Cadeby, near Market Bosworth, in May 1969, having participated in a local road run. Organised road runs have become one of the most enjoyable aspects of the preservation movement during the past 30 years, being popular with engine crew members and enthusiasts alike.

Burrell Gold Medal tractor 3851 again, this time fully restored at Horsham 1972 and carrying the name "The Tinker". New in 1920 to Dorking Rural District Council, it was later absorbed into the fleet of Surrey County Council and ended its commercial life with E Longhurst & Sons Ltd of Epsom, before entering preservation with the late Claude Jessett of Hadlow Down, Sussex. Designed to haul one or two trucks, steam tractors were popular for light haulage being faster on the road than a standard traction engine. This particular example carries a replica, painted on its motion cover, of the gold medal awarded to the design following its victorious participation in the 1907 RAC Road Trials.

During the 1920s, a new design of fairground ride, known as the Scenic Railway, was introduced to the tobers, a large, ornately decorated affair which required considerably more electricity to enable it to be operated and more powerful engines to haul it from place to place. Burrells of Thetford designed their 'Special Scenic' showman's road locomotive especially for the job. Rated at 8nhp, it carried a second dynamo, known as an 'exciter', mounted between chimney and cylinder block, which was used to boost the electricity generated when starting the ride. The 'cars' in which the punters rode on these scenic railways were very big, built from exquisitely carved wood and decorated with gold leaf. They were made to resemble such things as dragons, dolphins and whales. These cars were hoisted on and off the ride by the 'Special Scenic' engines, using a crane and lift mounted at the rear of the engine. Burrell 3887 "The Prince of Wales", illustrated, was new in 1922 to Henry Jennings & Sons of Devizes, Wilts and worked with their Whale Scenic Railway. The 18-ton engine has been in preservation since the 1950s and is pictured at Horsham in 1970.

A further example of a 6nhp Ransomes Sims & Jefferies compound traction engine, this one being 41046, built in 1930 and new to R F Fenn of Frating, Essex. It was acquired for preservation by Dick Martino, who at the time lived at Halstead, Essex, and consequently became one of the founder-engines of the East Anglian Traction Engine Club in 1955. The engine later moved to Berkshire and then, via London, to Sussex, being pictured at Horsham Rally in September 1970. Here, also, threshing is taking place in the background. Such working demonstrations are an essential part of the rally scene as they allow the general public to see the type of work for which a particular class of engine was once used.

The firm of Ruston, Proctor & Co Ltd had its factory at Lincoln and manufactured many types of engine, including this 5nhp single cylinder traction engine which was designated their Class SH. This 8.5-ton example was new to W Birch, Tilmanstone, Kent and spent the whole of its life working in this corner of England. Many of its preservation years have also been in the south east and the engine is pictured at Horsham in September 1972. A spark arrester is fitted to the chimney in order to trap any hot embers and so reduce fire risk.

BRITISH ROAD STEAM VEHICLES

MUSEUMS FEATURING COLLECTIONS OF STEAM ROAD VEHICLES

There are many museums throughout the British Isles which feature among their exhibits a number of steam road vehicles. Although a complete listing is not possible in this publication, a number of these museums in varied locations follows. Times of opening should be verified with the individual museum.

Amberley Museum, Houghton Bridge, Amberley, West Sussex.
Beamish Open Air Museum, Beamish, Stanley, Co. Durham.
Bressingham Steam Museum, Bressingham, Diss, Norfolk.
British Commercial Vehicle Museum, King Street, Leyland, Lancs.
The Charles Burrell Museum, Minstergate, Thetford, Norfolk.
Country Life Museum, Sandy Bay, Exmouth, Devon.
Dingle's Steam Village, Milford, Lifton, Devon.
Glasgow Museum of Transport, Kelvin Hall, Glasgow.

Hollycombe Steam Collection, Iron Hill, Hollycombe, West Sussex.
Levens Hall Steam Collection, Levens Hall, Kendal, Combria.
Long Shop Museum, Main Street, Leiston, Suffolk.
Museum of East Anglian Life, Stowmarket, Suffolk.
Museum of Lincolnshire Life, Burton Road, Lincoln.
National Motor Museum, Beaulieu, Brockenhurst, Hants.
Pallot Heritage Steam Museum, Trinity, Jersey, Channel Islands.
Science Museum Reserve Collection, Wroughton, Swindon, Wilts.
Strumpshaw Hall Steam Collection, Strumpshaw, Norwich, Norfolk.
Summerlee Heritage Trust, West Canal Street, Coatbridge, Lanarkshire.
Thursford Collection, Thursford, Fakenham, Norfolk.
Ulster Folk & Transport Museum, Cultra Manor, Holywood, Co. Down.
The Village, Fleggburgh, Great Yarmouth, Norfolk.

ESTABLISHED ANNUAL STEAM RALLIES & SHOWS

Well over 100 steam rallies of varying size and format are staged annually. The following list details just some of the more prominent established events which are staged from April to September each year in different parts of the British Isles:

April
Camborne Trevithick Day, Camborne Town Centre, Cornwall (last Saturday of month).

May
Rushden Historic Transport Rally, Higham Ferrers, Northants (May Day Weekend).
Lancashire Traction Engine Club Rally, Flixton, Manchester (May Day Weekend).
Newbury Steam Funtasia, Newbury Showground, Berks. (May Day Weekend).
Stoke Goldington Rally, Stoke Goldington, Bucks. (mid-May).
Tallington Steam & Country Festival, Tallington, Stamford, Lincs. (Mid-May).
Strumpshaw Steam Rally, Strumpshaw Hall, Norwich, Norfolk (Spring B H Weekend).
Sellindge Steam Special, Sellindge, Ashford, Kent (Spring B H Weekend).
Carrington Rally, Carrington, Boston, Lincs. (Spring B H Weekend).
ONCA Steam Rally, Thoresby Park, Ollerton, Notts. (Spring B H Weekend).
South Wales Steam & Vintage Rally, Abergavenny, Gwent. (Spring B H Weekend).

June
Upton Steam & Vintage Rally, Upton, Innishannon, Co Cork, Eire (early June).
Hertfordshire Steam Engine Club Rally, Leighton Buzzard, Beds. (early June).
South Tyne Traction Engine Society Rally, Stamfordham, Northumberland (early June).
Morcambe Bay Traction Engine Club Rally, St Michael's, Preston, Lancs. (mid-June).
Parham Steam Rally, Parham Park, Storrington, West Sussex (mid-June).
Bon Accord Steam Engine Club Rally, Hazelhead Park, Aberdeen (late June).
Sheffield & District Steam Society Rally, North Anston, Sheffield (late June).
Banbury Steam Society Rally, Bloxham, Banbury, Oxon. (late June).

July
Chiltern Traction Engine Club Rally, Prestwood, Great Missenden, Bucks. (early July).
Great Yorkshire Traction Engine Club Rally, Duncombe Park, Helmsley, N. Yorks. (early July).
Bromyard Gala Society Rally, Bromyard, Hereford (early July).
Hollowell Steam Rally, Hollowell, Northampton (early July).
Elvaston Steam Rally, Elvaston Castle, Derby (early July).
Rempstone Steam & Country Show, Wymeswold, Loughborough, Leics. (mid-July).
Woodcote Rally, Woodcote, South Oxon. (mid-July).
Cheshire Steam Fair, Grappenhall, Warrington, Ches. (mid-July).
Weeting Steam Engine Rally, Weeting, Brandon, Suffolk (mid-July)
Masham Steam Engine Rally, Low Burton, Masham, N Yorks. (July).

Herefordshire Traction Engine Club Rally, Much Marcle, Ledbury, Herefords. (mid-July).
Somerset Traction Engine Club Rally, Langport, Somerset (mid-July).
Ross-on-Wye Steam Engine Society Rally, Welland, Upton-upon-Severn, Worcs. (end July).
Cumbria Steam Society Rally, Flookburgh, Grange-over-Sands, Cumbria (end July).
Chester-le-Street Traction Engine Rally, Chester-le-Street, Co Durham (end July).

August
Pickering Traction Engine Rally, Pickering, N. Yorks. (early August).
Great Bucks Steam Working, Near Aylesbury, Bucks. (early August).
Irish Steam Preservation Society Rally, Stradbally, Co. Laoise, Eire (early August).
Astle Park Traction Engine Rally, Astle Park, Chelford, Ches. (mid-August).
Knowl Hill Hill Steam & Country Show, Knowl Hill, Reading, Berks. (mid-August).
East Riding Engine Club Rally, Driffield, E. Yorks. (mid-August).
West of England Steam Engine Society Rally, St. Agnes, Cornwall (mid-August).
Fairford Steam Rally & Show, Fairford, Glos. (mid-August).
Lincolnshire Steam Society Rally, Lincoln Showground (mid-August).
Leeds & District Steam Engine Club Rally, Harrogate, N. Yorks. (Late Summer B H).
Festival of Transport, Hellingly, Hailsham, Sussex (Late Summer B H).
Devon Traction Engine Club Rally, Chapelton, Barnstaple, N. Devon (Late Summer B H).
Honiton Hill Rally, Near Honiton, Devon (Late Summer B H).
County of Salop Steam Society Rally, Onslow Park, Shrewsbury, Salop. (late Summer B H)

September
Great Dorset Steam Fair, Tarrant Hinton, Blandford Forum, Dorset (early Sept).
Haddenham Steam Rally, Haddenham, Near Ely, Cambs. (early Sept).
Malpas Yesteryear Rally, Hampton, Malpas, Ches. (early Sept).
Essex Steam Rally, Barleylands, Billericay, Essex. (mid-Sept).
Bedford Steam Club Rally, Old Warden Park, Biggleswade, Beds. (mid-Sept).
Hanbury Steam Rally, Hanbury, Near Bromsgrove, Worcs. (late Sept).
Henham Steam Rally, Henham, Beccles, Suffolk (late Sept).
Power of the Past Rally, Wantisden, Woodbridge, Suffolk (late Sept).

A complete list of shows featuring road steam vehicles is a regular feature of the "preservation press". The following publications, available from newsagents, may be of interest to anyone wishing to obtain further details of such events:

'The World's Fair', a newspaper featuring regular preservation pages, published weekly 'Old Glory', a glossy magazine featuring all aspects of preservation, published monthly.

The National Traction Engine Trust publishes a quarterly magazine 'Steaming', which is distributed quarterly to all members and which features articles, news and event dates. Further information may be obtained by sending an S.A.E. to John R Cook, Dolfarni, Church Lane, Kirby-la-Thorpe, Sleaford, Lincs, NG34 9NH.